Baby Girl 2nd Year Memory Book

A toddler journal with plenty of space for photos and memories

Children are unpredictable. You never know what inconsistency they're going to catch you in next. ~Franklin P. Jones

A journal to document
your toddler's life as it happens!

A child can ask questions that a wise man cannot answer

Copyright © 2015
By Debbie Miller

Baby memory books at babyfirstyearbooks.com
Original dog baby books at dogjournals.com

"The fundamental job of a toddler is to rule the universe.
~Lawrence Kutner

The toddler craves independence, but he fears desertion.
~Dorothy Corkille Briggs

We worry about what a child will become tomorrow,
yet we forget that he is someone today.
~Stacia Tauscher

You can learn many things from children.
How much patience you have, for instance.
~Franklin P. Jones

"While we try to teach our children all about life,
Our children teach us what life is all about."
~Angela Schwindt

What you do with him can influence not only him, but everyone he meets
and not for a day or a month or a year, but for time and eternity."
~Rose Kennedy

All kids need is a little help, a little hope and
somebody who believes in them."
~Magic Johnson

"Cleaning your house while your kids are still growing up is
like shoveling the walk before it stops snowing."
~Phyllis Diller

Our Family Tree

Christiana Rayne Hazzard

Our Toddler

_____   Payton Ryland Hazzard

_____   _____

_____   _____

Sisters   Brothers

Tiana Hazzard   Chris Hazzard

Mommy   Daddy

Marianna Foxwell   Dawn Hazzard

Grandma   Grandma

Stan Foxwell   Paul Hazzard

Grandpa   Grandpa

SPECIAL TODDLER MOMENTS

SPECIAL TODDLER MOMENTS

FUNNY THINGS MY TODDLER SAID

My Toddler's Favorite Things

POTTY TRAINING DETAILS

_____

_____

_____

_____

_____

_____

_____

MY TODDLER'S FIRST STEPS

Photo Here

_____

_____

_____

MY TODDLER'S FIRST HAIRCUT

Photo Here

FIRST TODDLER ACHIEVEMENT

Photo Here

_____

_____

_____

BATH TIME

Photo Here

FAVORITE FOODS

_____

_____

_____

SLEEPING HABITS

_____

_____

_____

The littlest feet make the
biggest footprints in our hearts!

OUR TODDLER
13 MONTHS OLD

13 Months Old

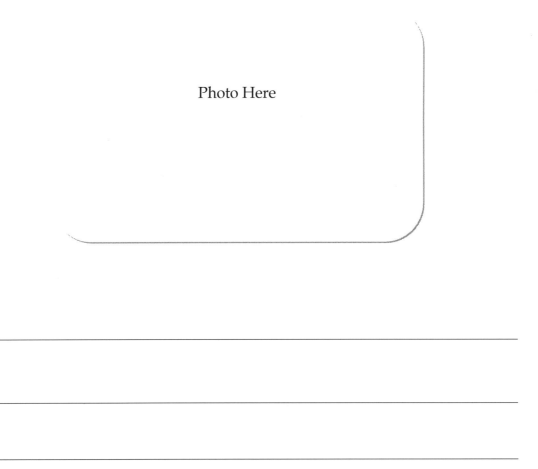

Photo Here

13 Months Old

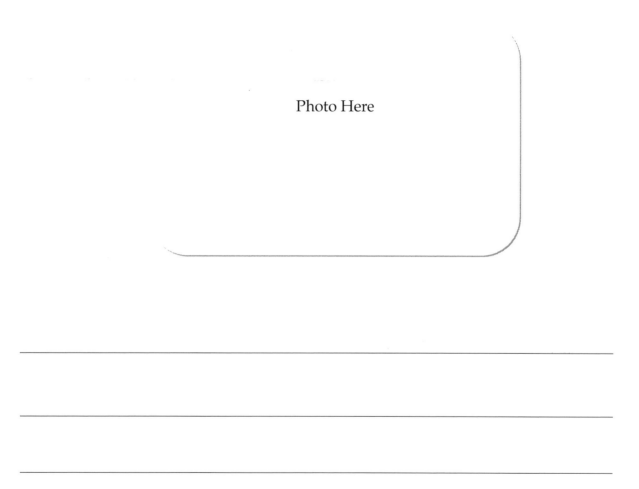

Photo Here

13 Months Old

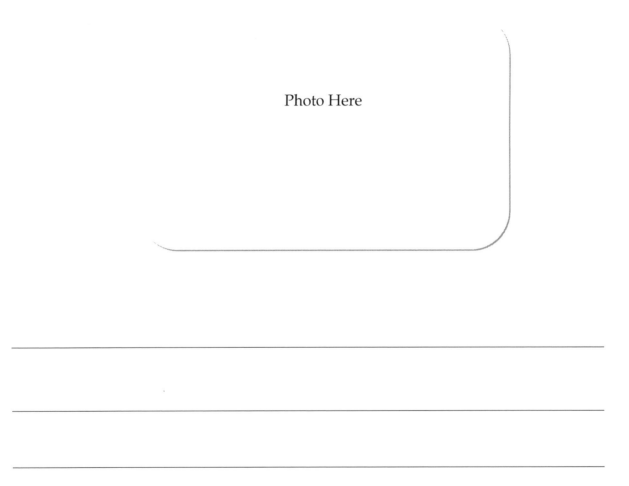

Photo Here

13 Months Old

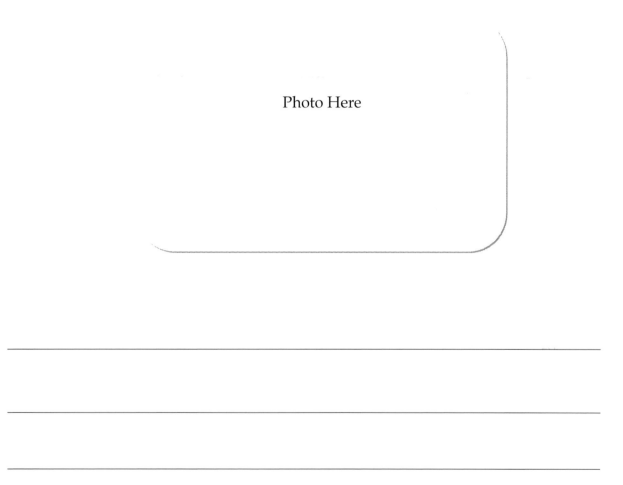

Photo Here

OUR TODDLER
14 MONTHS OLD

14 Months Old

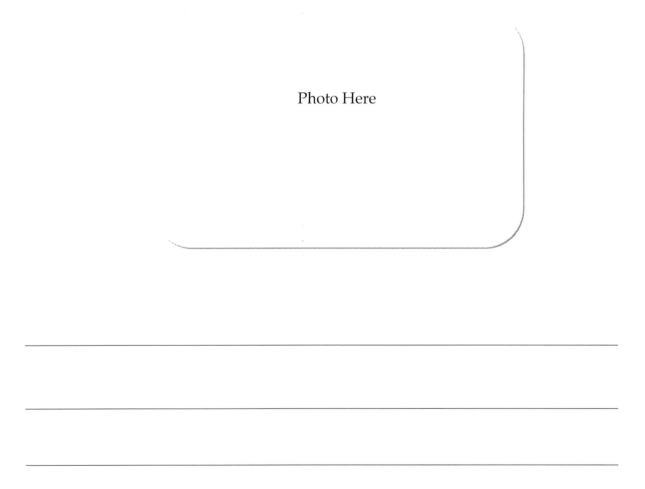

Photo Here

14 Months Old

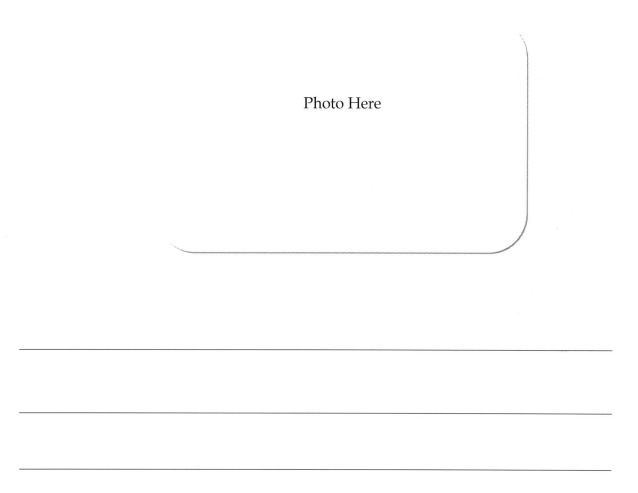

Photo Here

14 Months Old

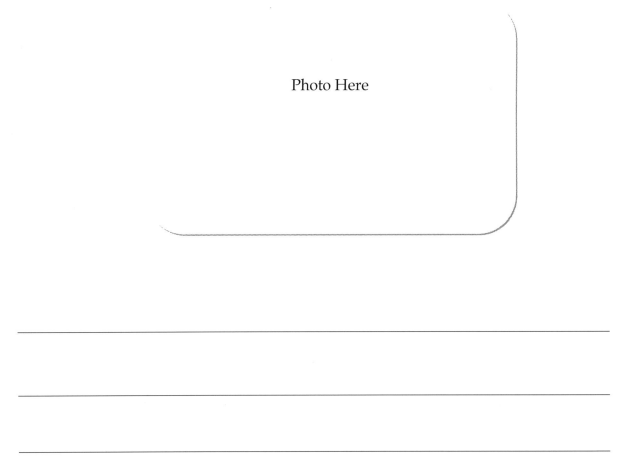

Photo Here

14 Months Old

Photo Here

OUR TODDLER
15 MONTHS OLD

15 Months Old

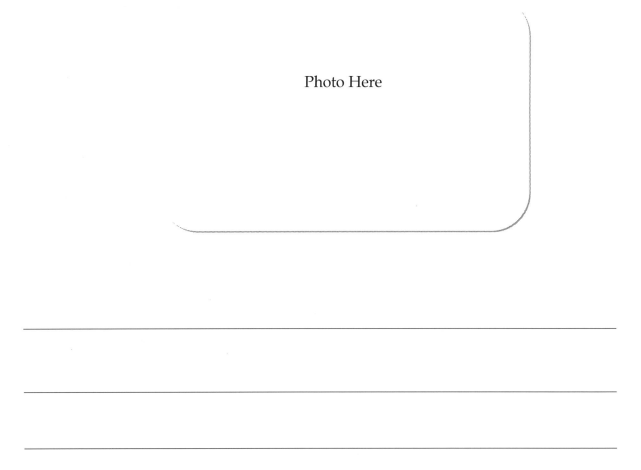

Photo Here

15 Months Old

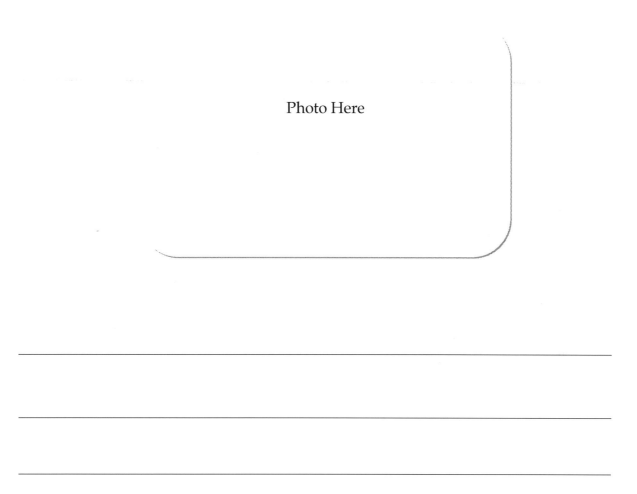

Photo Here

15 Months Old

Photo Here

15 Months Old

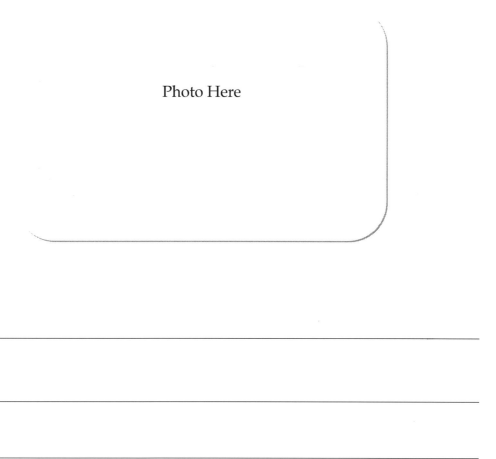

Photo Here

OUR TODDLER
16 MONTHS OLD

16 Months Old

Photo Here

16 Months Old

Photo Here

16 Months Old

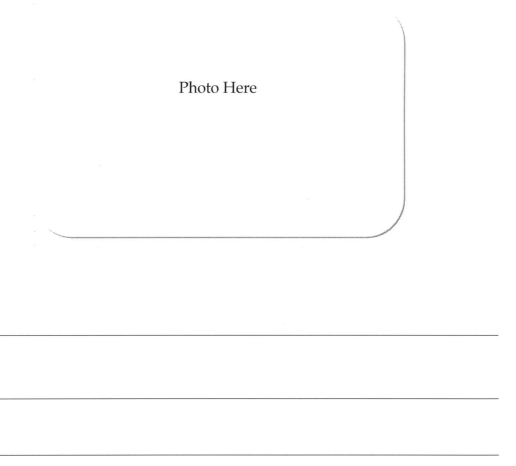

Photo Here

16 Months Old

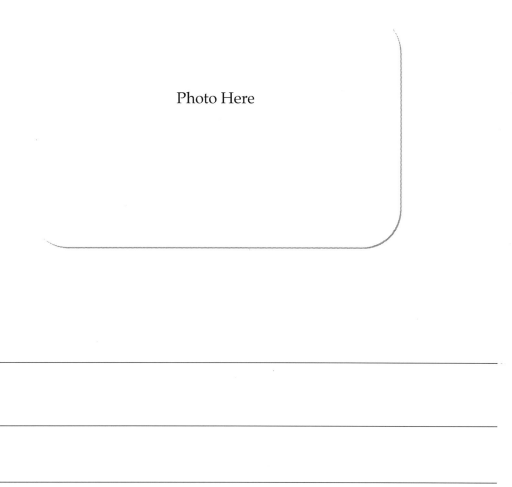

Photo Here

Our Toddler
17 Months Old

17 Months Old

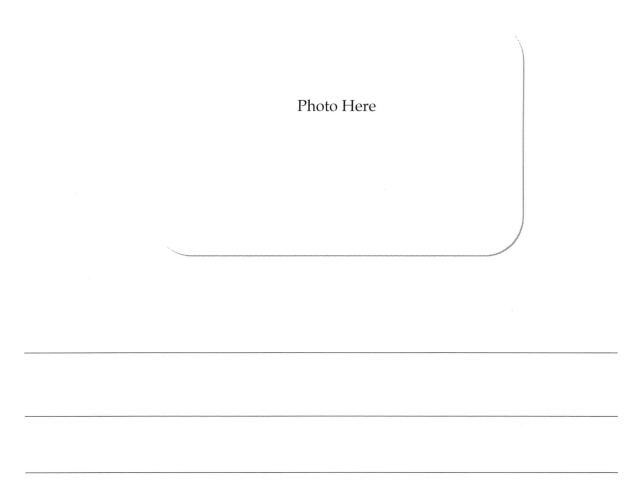

Photo Here

17 Months Old

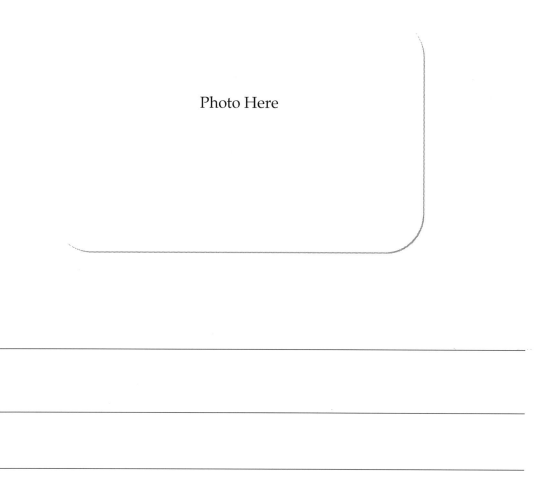

Photo Here

17 Months Old

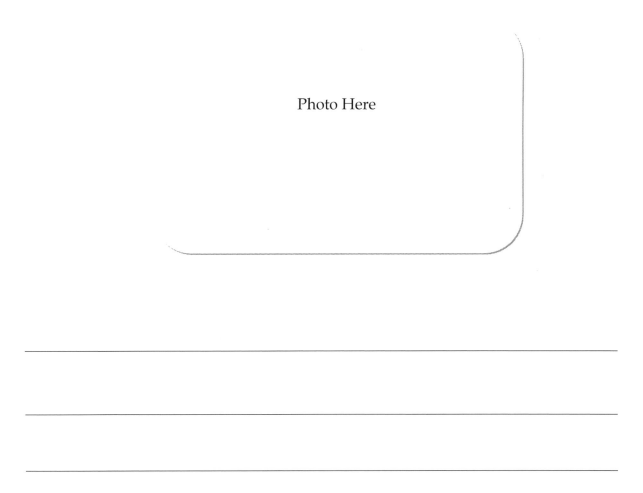

Photo Here

17 Months Old

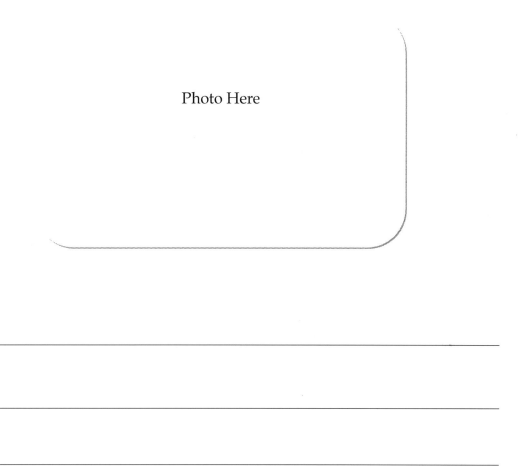

Photo Here

Our Toddler
18 Months Old

18 Months Old

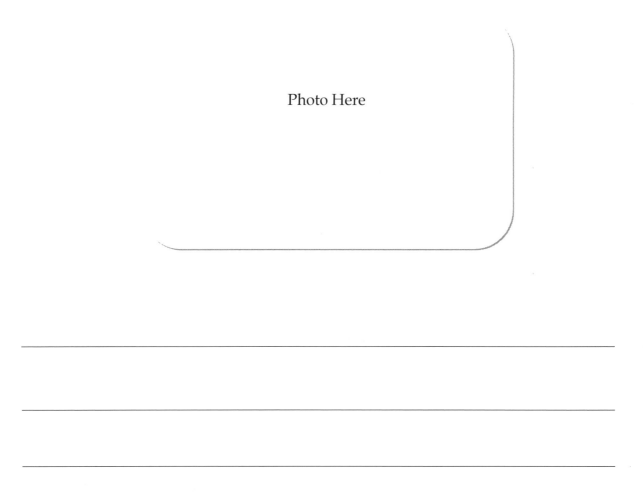

Photo Here

18 Months Old

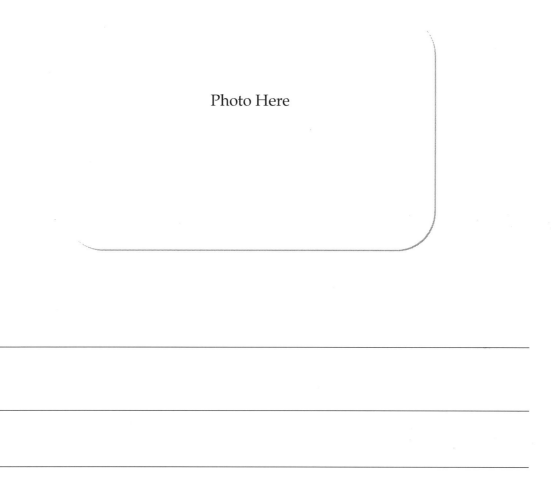

Photo Here

18 Months Old

Photo Here

18 MONTHS OLD

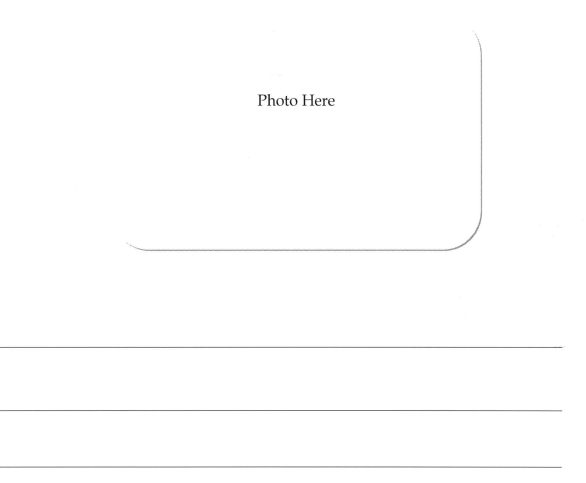

Photo Here

Our Toddler
19 Months Old

19 MONTHS OLD

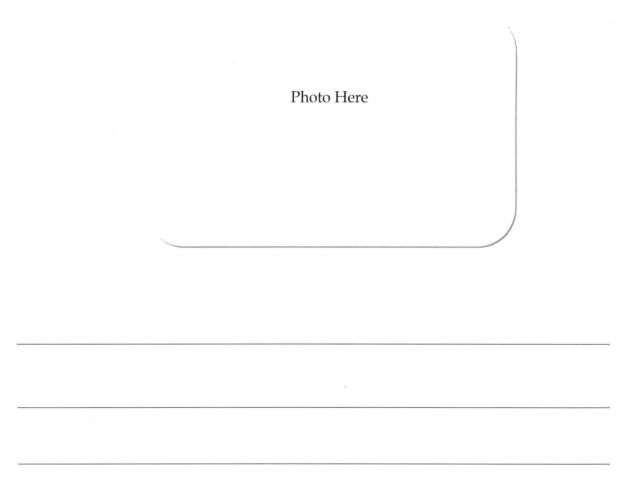

Photo Here

19 Months Old

Photo Here

19 Months Old

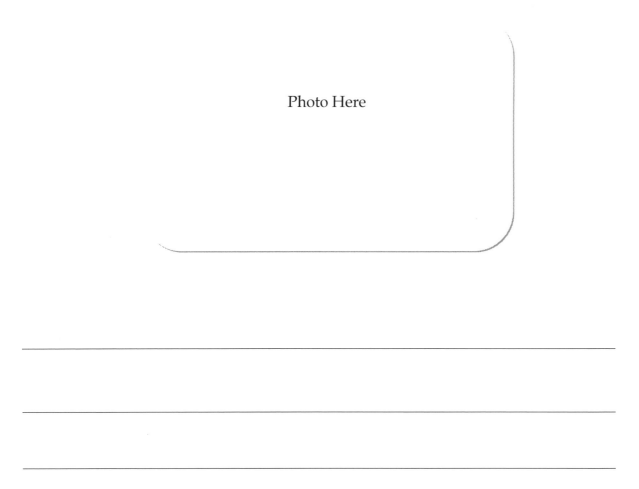

Photo Here

19 Months Old

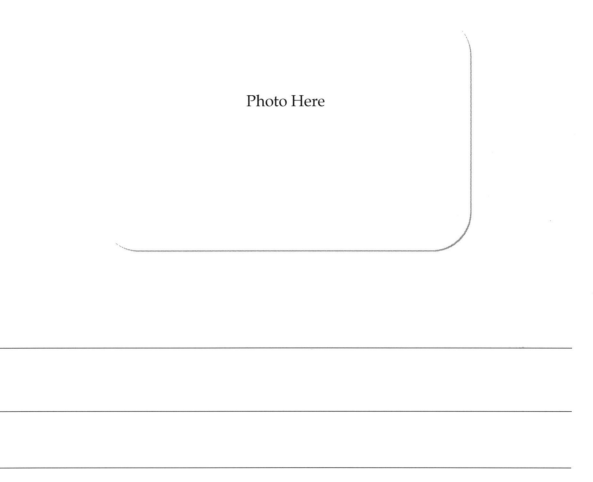

Photo Here

Our Toddler

20 MONTHS OLD

20 Months Old

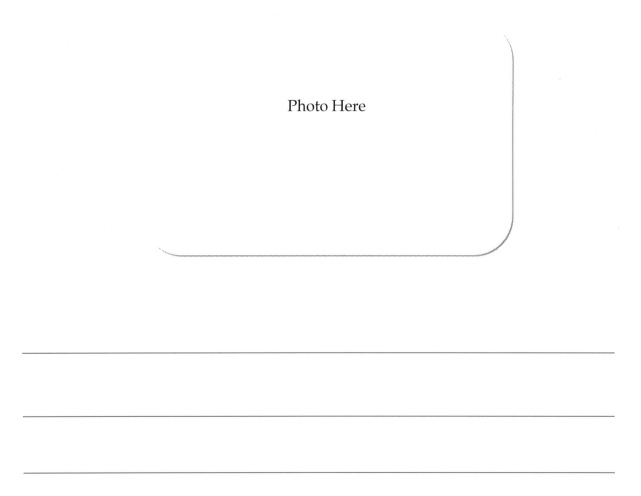

Photo Here

20 Months Old

Photo Here

20 Months Old

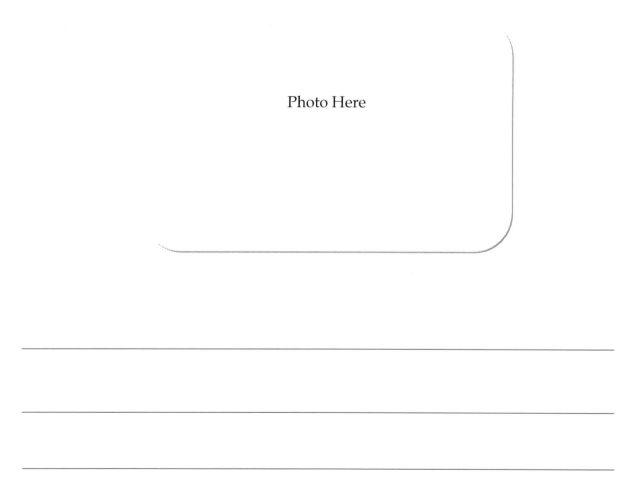

Photo Here

20 Months Old

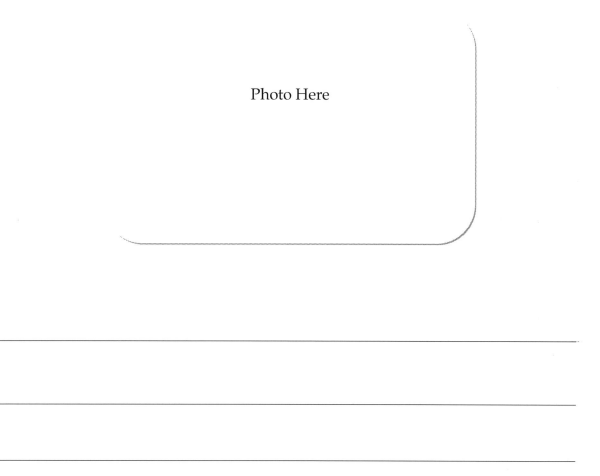

Photo Here

Our Toddler
21 Months Old

21 Months Old

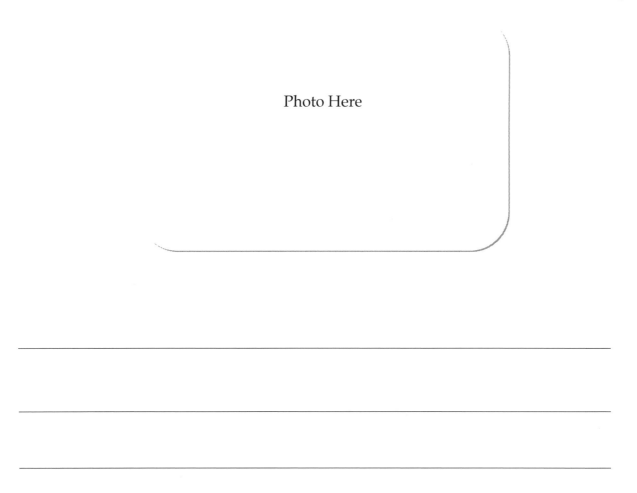

Photo Here

21 Months Old

Photo Here

21 Months Old

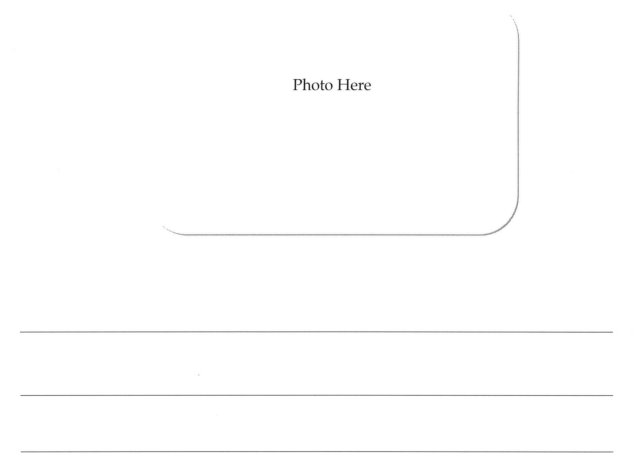

Photo Here

21 Months Old

Photo Here

Our Toddler
22 Months Old

22 Months Old

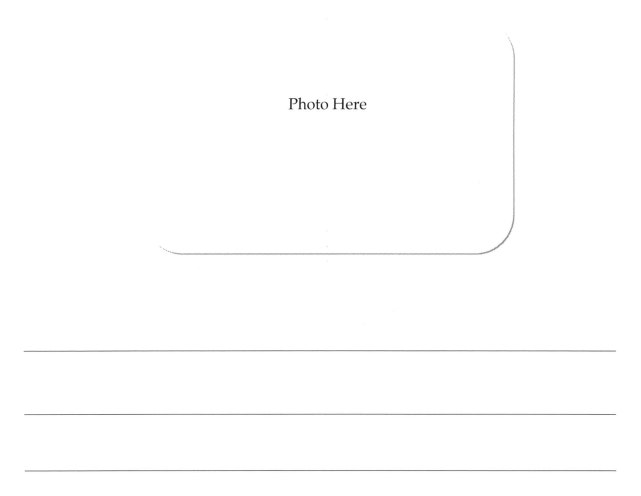

Photo Here

22 Months Old

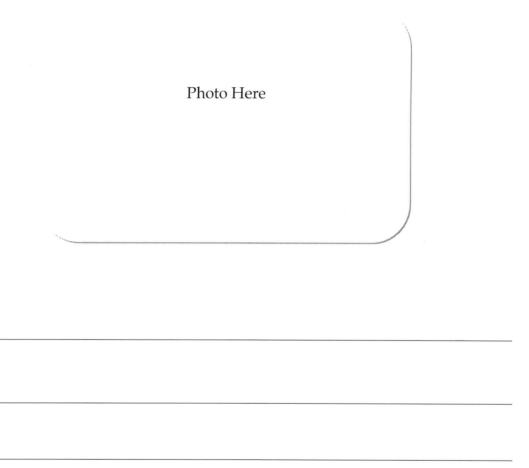

Photo Here

22 Months Old

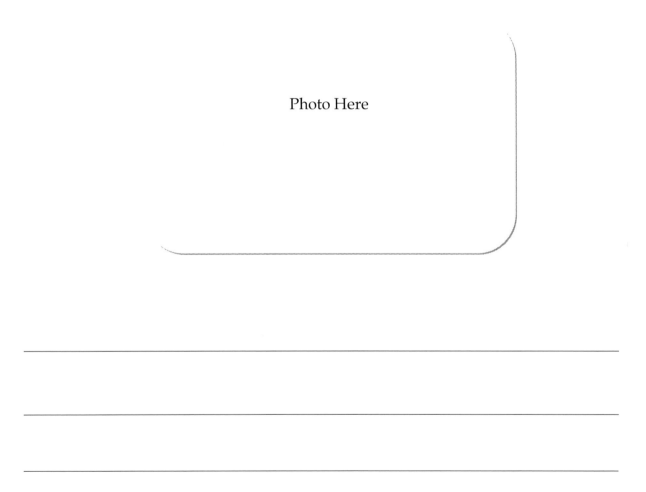

Photo Here

22 Months Old

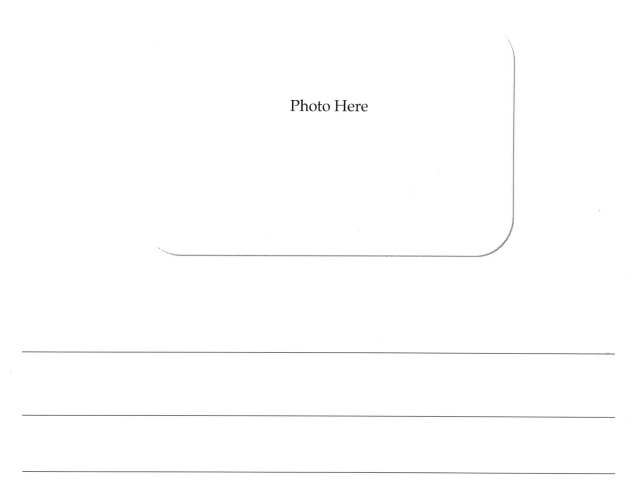

Photo Here

Our Toddler
23 Months Old

23 Months Old

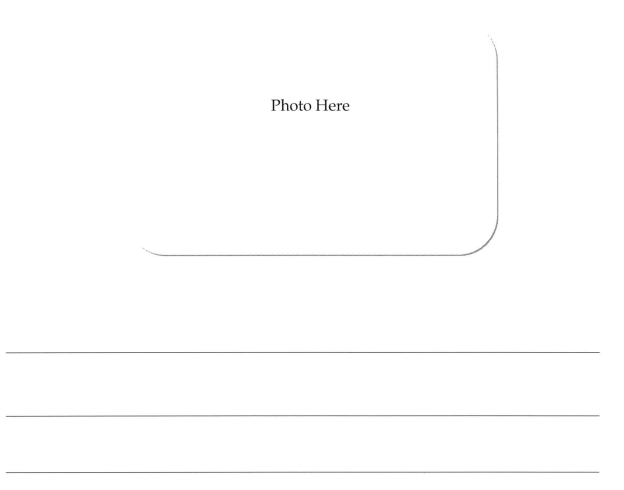

Photo Here

23 Months Old

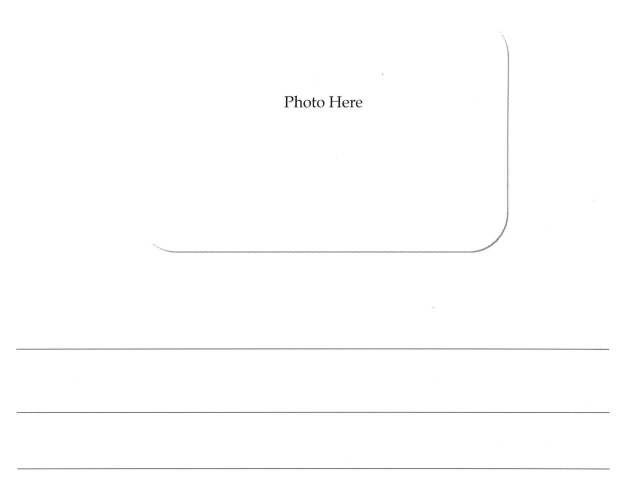

Photo Here

23 Months Old

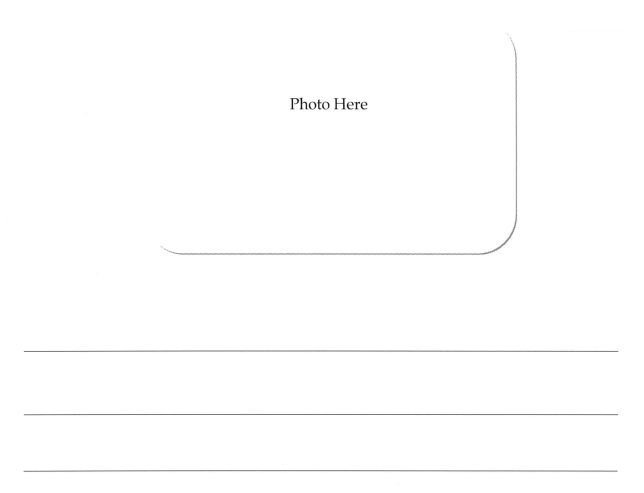

Photo Here

23 Months Old

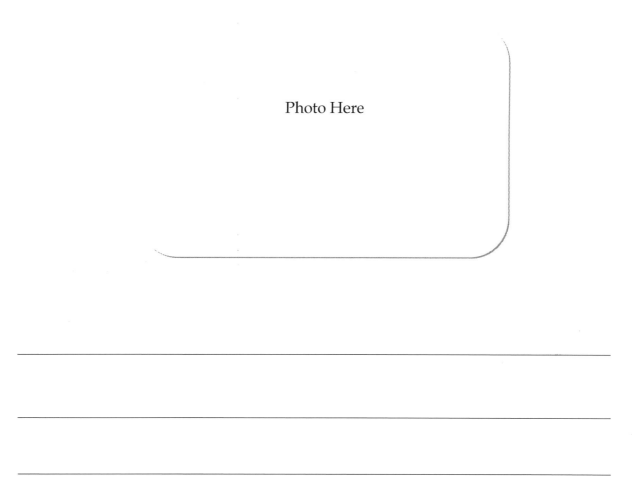

Photo Here

Our Toddler
24 Months Old

24 Months Old

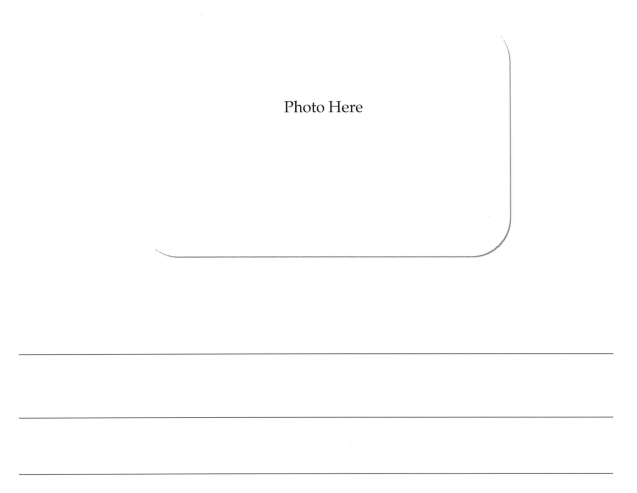

Photo Here

24 Months Old

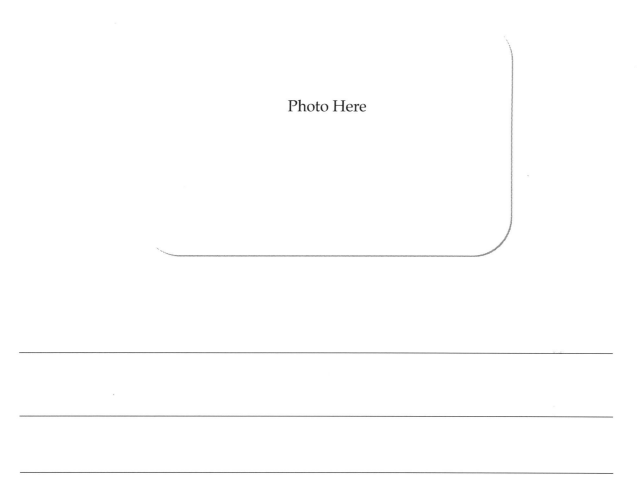

Photo Here

24 Months Old

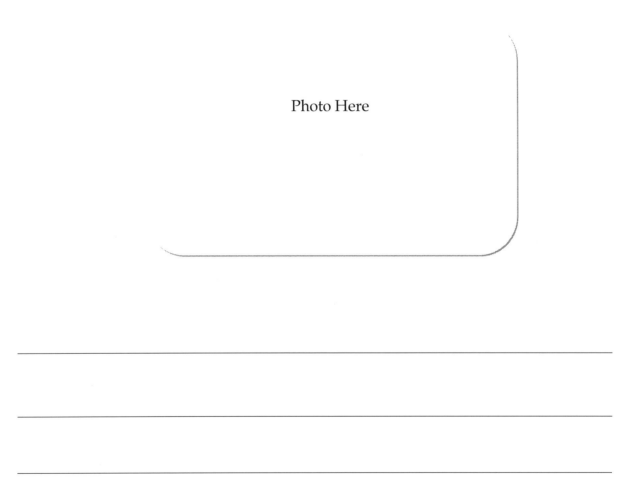

Photo Here

24 Months Old

Photo Here

Our Toddler
25 Months Old

25 Months Old

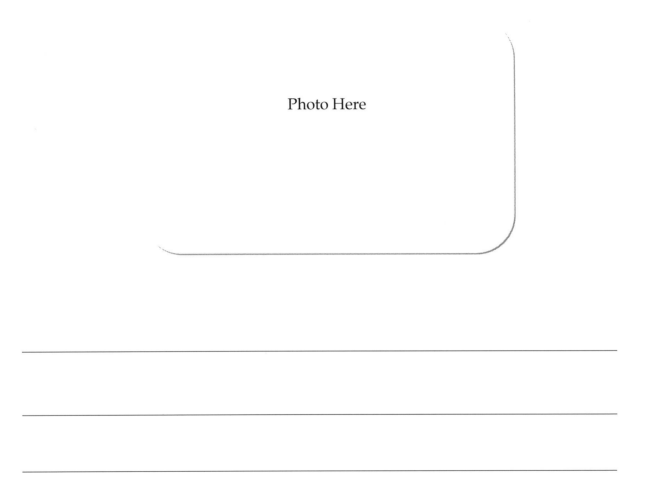

Photo Here

25 Months Old

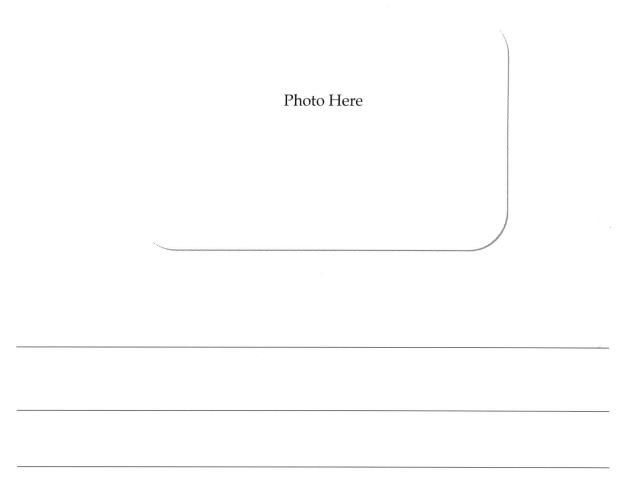

Photo Here

25 Months Old

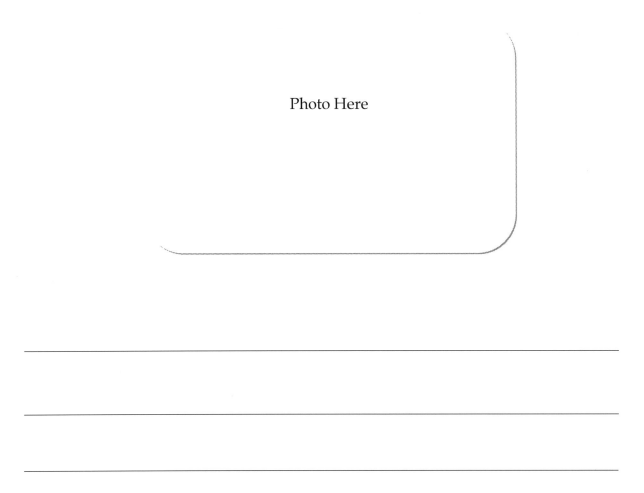

Photo Here

25 Months Old

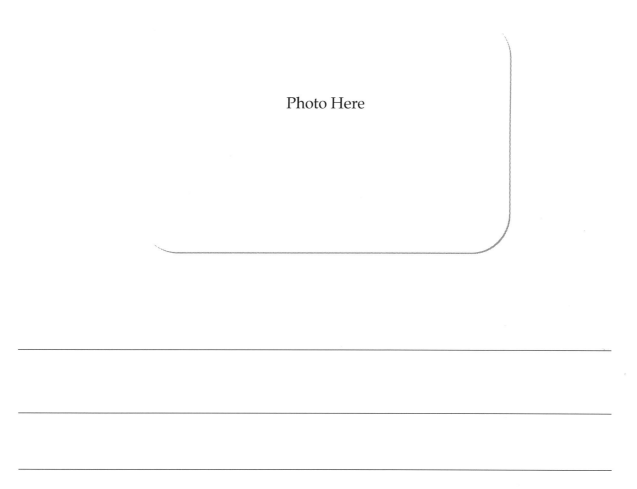

Photo Here

Our Toddler
26 MONTHS OLD

26 Months Old

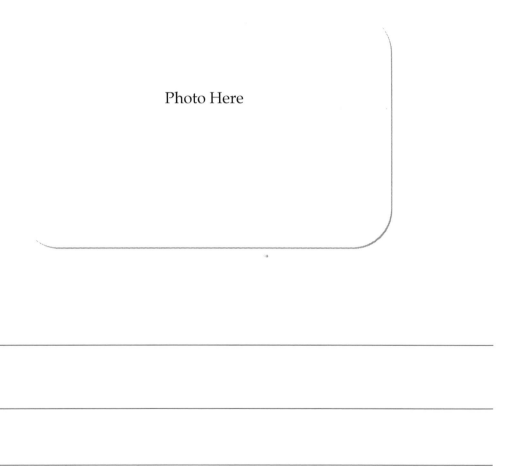

Photo Here

26 Months Old

Photo Here

26 Months Old

Photo Here

26 Months Old

Photo Here

_____

_____

_____

Our Toddler
27 Months Old

27 Months Old

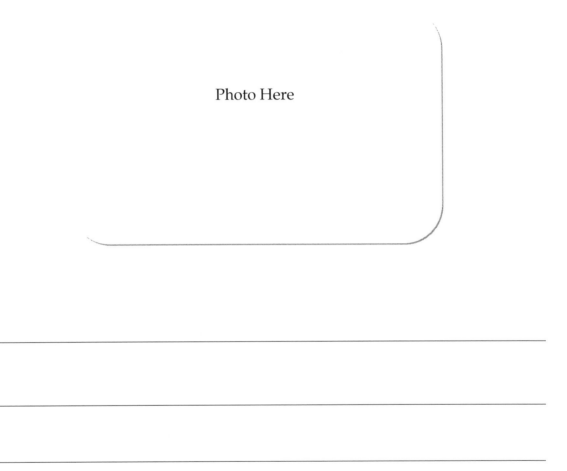

Photo Here

27 Months Old

Photo Here

27 Months Old

Photo Here

27 Months Old

Photo Here

Our Toddler
28 Months Old

28 Months Old

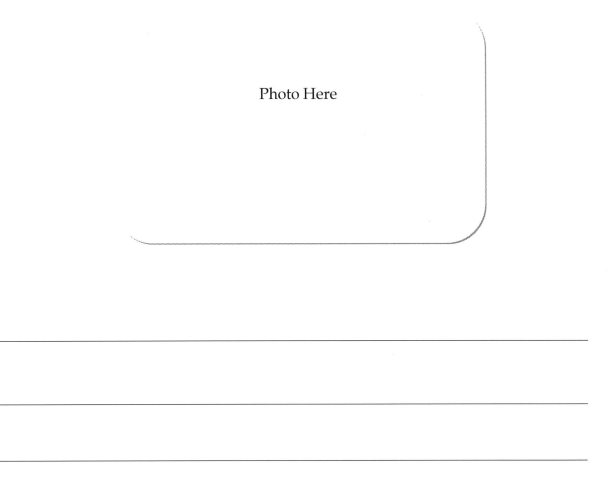

Photo Here

28 Months Old

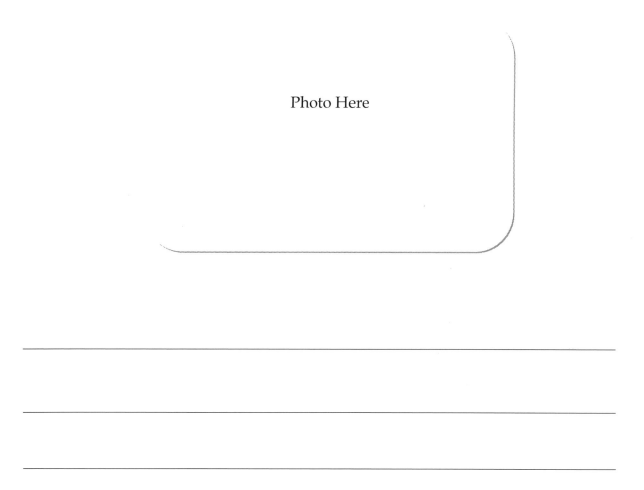

Photo Here

28 Months Old

Photo Here

28 Months Old

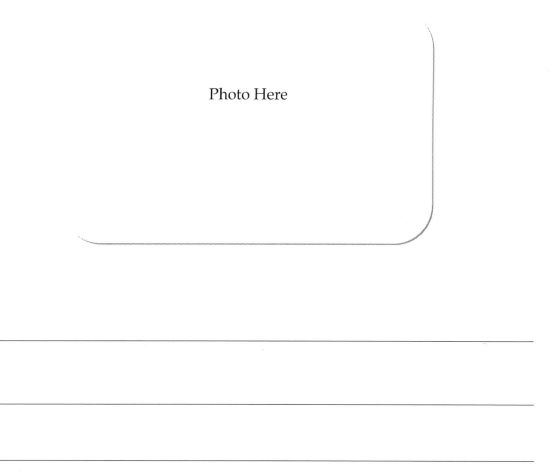

Photo Here

_____

_____

_____

Memories and Milestones
Don't Miss The Happy Moments

Age: _____

Date: _____**Where:** _____

Photo Here

_____

_____

_____

Age: _____

Date: _____**Where:** _____

Photo Here

Age: _____

Date: _____**Where:** _____

Photo Here

Age: _____

Date: _____**Where:** _____

Photo Here

Age: _____

Date: _____**Where:** _____

Photo Here

Age: _____

Date: _____**Where:** _____

Photo Here

_____

_____

_____

Age: _____

Date: _____**Where:** _____

Photo Here

_____

_____

_____

Age: _____

Date: _____**Where:** _____

Photo Here

_____

_____

_____

Age: _____

Date: _____**Where:** _____

Photo Here

Age: _____

Date: _____**Where:** _____

Photo Here

Age: _____

Date: _____**Where:** _____

Photo Here

_____

_____

_____

Age: _____

Date: _____ **Where:** _____

```
┌─────────────────────────────┐
│                             │
│                             │
│                             │
│         Photo Here          │
│                             │
│                             │
│                             │
└─────────────────────────────┘
```

_____

_____

_____

Age: _____

Date: _____**Where:** _____

```
┌─────────────────────────────────┐
│                                 │
│                                 │
│                                 │
│          Photo Here             │
│                                 │
│                                 │
│                                 │
└─────────────────────────────────┘
```

_____

_____

_____

Age: _____

Date: _____ **Where:** _____

```
+---------------------------------+
|                                 |
|                                 |
|                                 |
|           Photo Here            |
|                                 |
|                                 |
|                                 |
+---------------------------------+
```

_____

_____

_____

Age: _____

Date: _____**Where:** _____

```
┌─────────────────────────────────┐
│                                 │
│                                 │
│                                 │
│            Photo Here           │
│                                 │
│                                 │
│                                 │
└─────────────────────────────────┘
```

_____

_____

_____

Age: _____

Date: _____**Where:** _____

Photo Here

_____

_____

_____

Age: _____

Date: _____**Where:** _____

Photo Here

Age: _____

Date: _____**Where:** _____

Photo Here

_____

_____

_____

Age: _____

Date: _____ **Where:** _____

```
┌─────────────────────────────────┐
│                                 │
│                                 │
│                                 │
│           Photo Here            │
│                                 │
│                                 │
│                                 │
│                                 │
└─────────────────────────────────┘
```

_____

_____

_____

Age: _____

Date: _____ **Where:** _____

Photo Here

Age: _____

Date: _____**Where:** _____

Photo Here

_____

_____

_____

Age: _____

Date: _____**Where:** _____

Photo Here

_____

_____

_____

Age: _____

Date: _____**Where:** _____

```
┌─────────────────────────────┐
│                             │
│                             │
│                             │
│         Photo Here          │
│                             │
│                             │
│                             │
└─────────────────────────────┘
```

_____

_____

_____

Age: _____

Date: _____**Where:** _____

Photo Here

_____

_____

_____

Age: _____

Date: _____**Where:** _____

Photo Here

_____

_____

_____

Age: _____

Date: _____**Where:** _____

Photo Here

Age: _____

Date: _____ **Where:** _____

Photo Here

_____

_____

_____

37578789R00080

Made in the USA
Columbia, SC
30 November 2018